THE SEVEN WONDERS OF THE MODERN WORLD

THE GREAT WALL OF CHINA

BLASTOFF! DISCOVERY

BY ELIZABETH NOLL

BELLWETHER MEDIA • MINNEAPOLIS, MN

Blastoff! Discovery launches a new mission: reading to learn. Filled with facts and features, each book offers you an exciting new world to explore!

This edition first published in 2021 by Bellwether Media, Inc.

No part of this publication may be reproduced in whole or in part without written permission of the publisher. For information regarding permission, write to Bellwether Media, Inc., Attention: Permissions Department, 6012 Blue Circle Drive, Minnetonka, MN 55343.

Library of Congress Cataloging-in-Publication Data

Names: Noll, Elizabeth, author.
Title: The Great Wall of China / by Elizabeth Noll.
Description: Minneapolis, MN : Bellwether Media, Inc., 2021. |
Series: Blastoff Discovery!: The Seven Wonders of the Modern World
  | Includes bibliographical references and index. | Audience: Ages
  7-13 | Audience: Grades 4-6 | Summary: "Engaging images
  accompany information about the Great Wall of China. The
  combination of high-interest subject matter and narrative text is
  intended for students in grades 3 through 8" – Provided by
  publisher.
Identifiers: LCCN 2020018894 (print) | LCCN 2020018895 (ebook)
  | ISBN 9781644872680 (library binding) | ISBN
  9781681037318 (ebook)
Subjects: LCSH: Great Wall of China (China)–Juvenile literature. | Civil
  engineering–China–History–Juvenile literature. | China–History–To
  221 B.C.–Juvenile literature. | Walls–China–Design and
  construction–History–Juvenile literature.
Classification: LCC DS793.G67 N65 2021 (print) | LCC DS793.
  G67 (ebook) | DDC 931–dc23
LC record available at https://lccn.loc.gov/2020018894

Editor: Betsy Rathburn   Designer: Brittany McIntosh

Printed in the United States of America, North Mankato, MN.

TABLE OF CONTENTS

CHINA'S LONG WALL

After a long bus ride from Beijing, you have finally arrived at your destination. Before today, you have only seen it in pictures. But now, you are standing atop the most famous wall in the world.

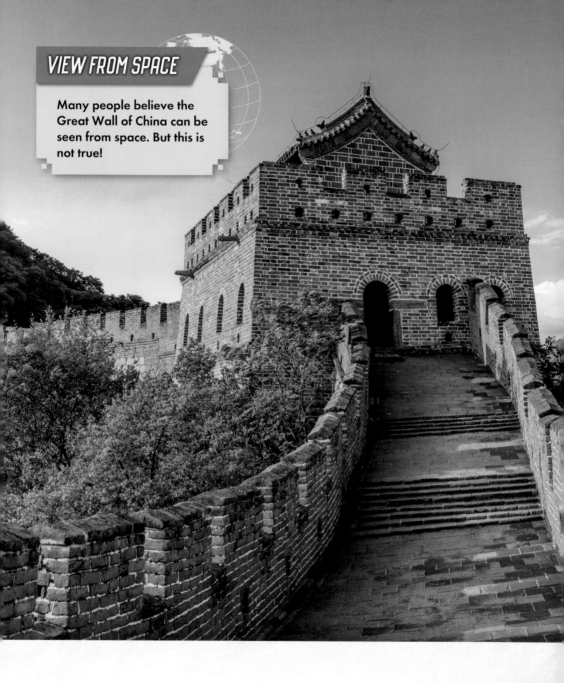

VIEW FROM SPACE

Many people believe the Great Wall of China can be seen from space. But this is not true!

The wall follows the curve of the land like the spine of an animal. Its stone structures dot the tree-covered hills around it. The wall stretches as far as your eye can see. This is the Great Wall of China!

5

EARTH AND STONE

The Great Wall of China stretches across thousands of miles of northern China. It is made up of many sections built over thousands of years. The most famous part was built from the 1300s to the 1600s during the Ming **dynasty**. The Ming wall's easternmost point is on a beach on the Yellow Sea. This part of the Great Wall stretches more than 5,000 miles (8,046 kilometers) into China.

Other sections cross diverse parts of China's landscape. The Yellow River and the Gobi Desert both hold parts of the Great Wall.

CROSSING THE BORDER

Part of the Great Wall is in present-day North Korea!

GOBI DESERT

The Great Wall is made up of many materials. Older parts of the wall are made from hard dirt. Dirt was piled into tall barriers. Then it was pounded firm until it was like cement. Parts of these dirt walls still stand today, thousands of years later!

WHERE IS THE GREAT WALL OF CHINA?

SECTIONS OF THE GREAT WALL

N
W E
S

WARRING STATES   QIN

HAN   NORTHERN WEI

NORTHERN QI, SUI   LIAO, JIN

MING

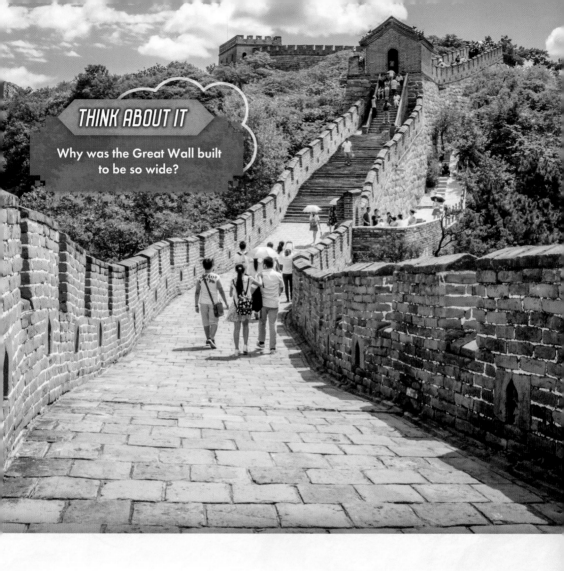

THINK ABOUT IT

Why was the Great Wall built to be so wide?

The newer Ming sections are mostly made of brick and stone. The stones were piled about 25 feet (8 meters) tall and 30 feet (9 meters) wide. In the widest sections, five horses can run side by side! Watchtowers and forts along the wall provided shelter to soldiers and guards.

WATCHTOWER

CENTURIES OF WALLS

For thousands of years, people in China built walls to protect farms, temples, and cities. Some rulers used walls to mark their borders. Many of these walls snaked across China. But they were not connected.

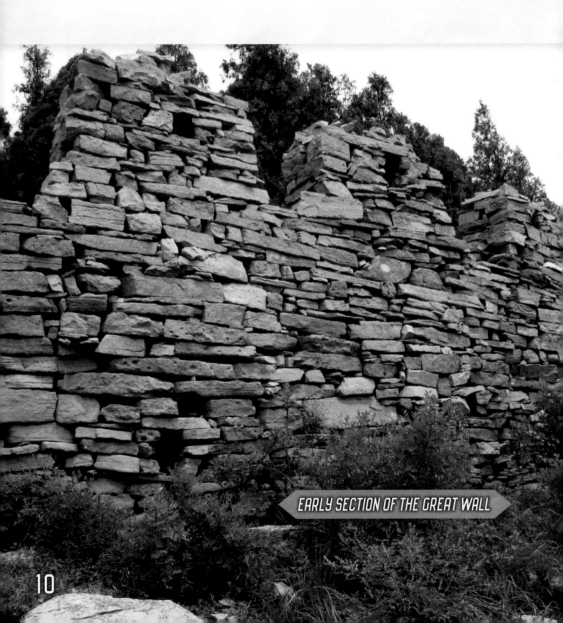

EARLY SECTION OF THE GREAT WALL

Things changed in 221 BCE. Emperor Qin took power, joining many smaller regions. The new nation was united. But there was still danger in the north. **Nomads** from Mongolia invaded the region. Qin decided to join some of the older walls together. This created a border meant to stop the raids. Soldiers waited in forts along the wall. They sent smoke signals if invaders were attacking!

11

Qin was a cruel leader. He forced hundreds of thousands of people to leave their homes to work on the wall. They barely had enough food to survive. They had to sleep on the ground with no shelter. Thousands of people died.

Still, workers had no choice but to continue. They built the wall using the **rammed earth**, or *hangtu*, method. First, builders filled a wooden frame with dirt and pounded it until it was hard. Once it was solid, they put another layer of dirt on top. They kept adding layers of dirt until they had a high wall.

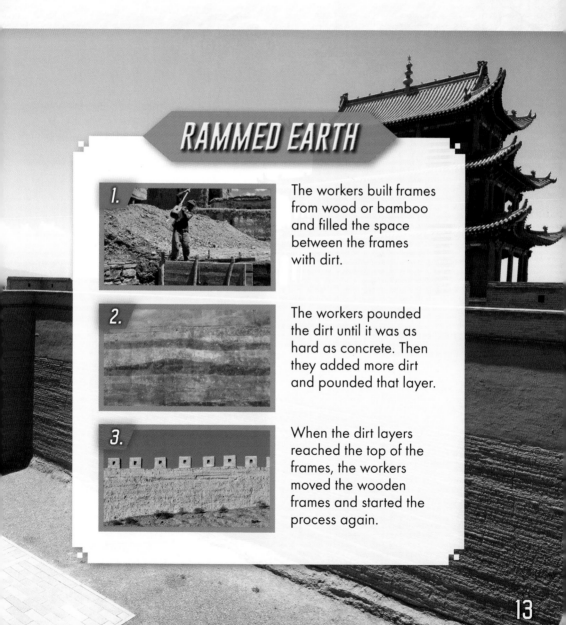

RAMMED EARTH

1. The workers built frames from wood or bamboo and filled the space between the frames with dirt.

2. The workers pounded the dirt until it was as hard as concrete. Then they added more dirt and pounded that layer.

3. When the dirt layers reached the top of the frames, the workers moved the wooden frames and started the process again.

Emperor Qin died in 206 BCE. A new emperor took over, and the Han dynasty began. The Han dynasty ruled China for more than 400 years. Han emperors repaired parts of Qin's wall. They added new sections, too. The wall was extended into the Gobi Desert in northern China.

HAN DYNASTY WALL

The desert brought new challenges. The builders still used the rammed earth method, but they had to use different materials. There were few trees, so workers used stems and branches to weave frames. The frames were filled with pounded sand and gravel. Parts of the desert wall still stand after more than 2,000 years!

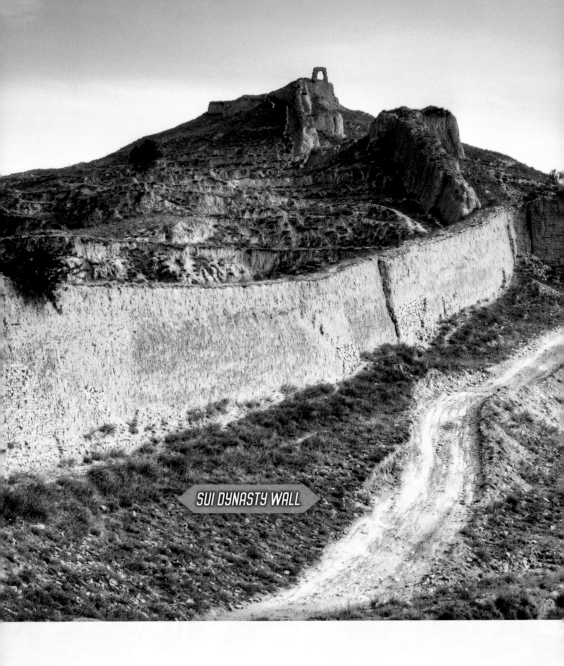

SUI DYNASTY WALL

After the Han dynasty ended, many groups struggled for control of China. The Sui dynasty found power in 581 CE. For almost 40 years, its emperors extended the Great Wall several times. It helped stop invaders. It also showed off the dynasty's power.

The Tang dynasty rose in 618. The dynasty's strong military meant the wall was not needed for protection. Soldiers walked along it to protect traders along the **Silk Road**. But work on the wall stopped for many years. Later dynasties added little to the wall. The Liao and Song dynasties used **trenches** to stop invaders.

GREAT WALL TIMELINE

221 BCE
Emperor Qin gains power and begins connecting ancient walls

206
Han dynasty begins, leading to new walls being built in different regions

581 CE
Sui dynasty builds new walls to show off China's power

618
Tang dynasty soldiers walk the wall to protect traders

1368
Ming dynasty starts first work on the Great Wall in over 700 years

1644
Work on the wall stops again with the Qing dynasty

2006
China creates laws to protect the Great Wall

THEN AND NOW

THEN

During the Ming dynasty, workers used windlasses to build the Great Wall. These were made from rope wrapped around wooden wheels. Workers turned the crank to lift heavy weights.

NOW

Today, work is done using heavy machines. Workers use levers to control the machines. They do not have to lift weight themselves!

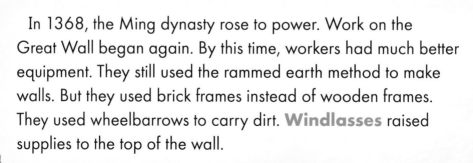

In 1368, the Ming dynasty rose to power. Work on the Great Wall began again. By this time, workers had much better equipment. They still used the rammed earth method to make walls. But they used brick frames instead of wooden frames. They used wheelbarrows to carry dirt. **Windlasses** raised supplies to the top of the wall.

Workers also learned how to make **mortar** to hold bricks together. They mixed limestone and water together. This special mortar helped the Great Wall outlast **erosion** and earthquakes.

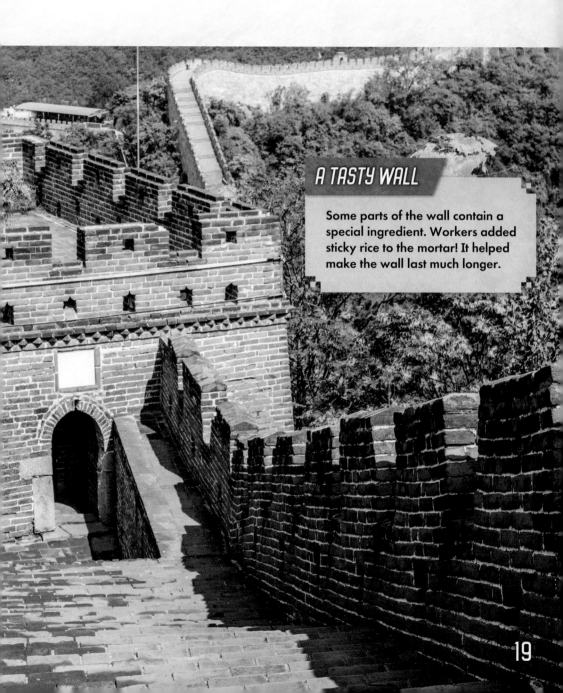

A TASTY WALL

Some parts of the wall contain a special ingredient. Workers added sticky rice to the mortar! It helped make the wall last much longer.

KEEPING UP THE WALL

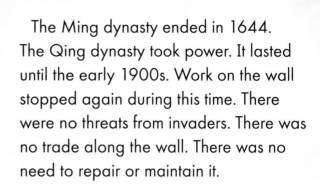

The Ming dynasty ended in 1644. The Qing dynasty took power. It lasted until the early 1900s. Work on the wall stopped again during this time. There were no threats from invaders. There was no trade along the wall. There was no need to repair or maintain it.

Without maintenance, the wall began to crumble. Weather caused erosion. Plants grew between the bricks. People took the bricks and stones to use for new buildings. In some places, farmers plowed right over the crumbling wall.

EROSION

THINK ABOUT IT

Today, the Great Wall marks only a small part of China's border. What is another way to mark a country's borders?

During the 1960s, damage to the wall grew. Chinese leaders decided that the Great Wall should be torn down. China's top leader, Mao Zedong, encouraged people to take apart the ancient wall. He told them to use the bricks to build houses and animal pens.

MAO ZEDONG

But about 20 years later, things changed again. Chinese leaders stopped trying to tear down the wall. Instead, they started repairing it. People around the world learned about the Great Wall, and **tourists** traveled to China to see it.

TOURISTS VISITING THE GREAT WALL

MANY WALLS, ONE COUNTRY

In 2007, the Great Wall of China was named a Wonder of the Modern World. More than 10 million people visit the Great Wall every year. It is one of the most popular sites in the world.

Most of these tourists visit the wall near Beijing. There, the wall is well preserved, and people can walk on top of it. But in other parts of China, the Great Wall is in ruins. In some areas, the wall is nothing more than a low mound of dirt.

New discoveries have been made at the Great Wall. **Archaeologists** have even found parts of the wall that no one knew about! They uncovered sections that had been covered by sand or eroded.

ARCHAEOLOGISTS VISITING A NEWLY DISCOVERED SECTION OF THE WALL

GREAT WALL OF CHINA

BERLIN WALL

LOCATION
China

LOCATION
Berlin, Germany

BUILT
221 BCE to 1644 CE

BUILT
August 13, 1961

MATERIALS
dirt, bricks, stone

MATERIALS
barbed wire, concrete

HEIGHT
more than 20 feet (6 meters)

HEIGHT
almost 12 feet (4 meters)

LENGTH
up to 13,000 miles
(20,921 kilometers)

LENGTH
96 miles (155 kilometers)

PURPOSE
protect from invasion

PURPOSE
separate East Berlin from
West Berlin

Many **artifacts** have been found at the wall, too. At one site, repair workers found chessboards and about 40 ancient chess pieces. The small, round chess pieces were made out of clay and carved with characters on top. The chess pieces were found at the base of an ancient watchtower. Maybe guards played chess 500 years ago at the base of the Great Wall!

In 2006, China created laws to protect the Great Wall. People are not allowed to take parts of the wall. It is also illegal to damage or write on the wall. Other protections will help stop damage from natural causes. A forest will be planted near the wall to protect it from wind. New rules could lower **pollution** and stop **acid rain** damage.

These rules will help, but the wall is still in danger. Some people still take pieces. Erosion still wears down the stones. But leaders hope their changes will keep the Great Wall of China safe for years to come. This modern wonder is an important piece of history!

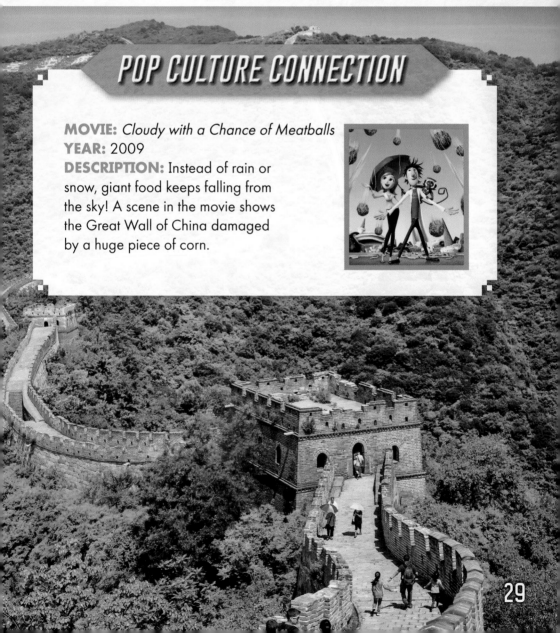

POP CULTURE CONNECTION

MOVIE: *Cloudy with a Chance of Meatballs*
YEAR: 2009
DESCRIPTION: Instead of rain or snow, giant food keeps falling from the sky! A scene in the movie shows the Great Wall of China damaged by a huge piece of corn.

GLOSSARY

acid rain—rain that contains chemicals from pollution; acid rain can damage buildings.

archaeologists—scientists who study things left behind by ancient people

artifacts—items made long ago by humans; artifacts tell people today about people from the past.

dynasty—a line of rulers that come from the same family

erosion—the process through which rocks are worn away by wind, water, ice, or human activity

mortar—a building material that hardens when it dries; mortar is used to fill cracks.

nomads—people who have no fixed home but wander from place to place

pollution—the presence of harmful materials in the environment

rammed earth—a building method in which dirt is pressed between two frames until it is solid

Silk Road—an ancient trade route that went from China to the Mediterranean Sea

tourists—people who travel to visit a place

trenches—long pits in the ground used for military defense

windlasses—machines used for lifting heavy objects; a windlass uses ropes over a wheel turned by a crank to lift objects.

TO LEARN MORE

AT THE LIBRARY

Demuth, Patricia. *Where is the Great Wall?* New York, N.Y.: Grosset & Dunlap, 2015.

Morley, Jacqueline. *You Wouldn't Want to Work on the Great Wall of China!* New York, N.Y.: Franklin Watts, 2017.

Oachs, Emily Rose. *Ancient China.* Minneapolis, Minn.: Bellwether Media, 2020.

ON THE WEB

FACTSURFER

Factsurfer.com gives you a safe, fun way to find more information.

1. Go to www.factsurfer.com.

2. Enter "Great Wall of China" into the search box and click Q.

3. Select your book cover to see a list of related content.

INDEX

The images in this book are reproduced through the courtesy of: aphotostory, front cover, pp. 3, 18 (bottom), 31; superjoseph, pp. 4-5, 27 (Great Wall); Leonid Andronov/ Alamy, p. 6; Ana Flašker/ Alamy, p. 7; zhao jiankang, pp. 8, 9 (bottom); Dutsadee, p. 9 (top); Rolfmueller/ Wikipedia, p. 10; Pan Hong/ Getty Images, p. 11; National Geographic Image Collection/ Alamy, p. 12; imageBROKER/ Alamy, p. 13 (step 1); Chayot Kiranantawat, p. 13 (step 2); rweisswald, p. 13 (step 3); Tom Salyer/ Alamy, p. 13 (bottom); SIHASAKPRACHUM, p. 14; Henry Westheim Photography/ Alamy, p. 15; Roberto Esposti/ Alamy, p. 16; Wang Sing, p. 17; Shawn Clovis, p. 18 (then); ZoranOrcik, p. 18 (now); aphotostory, p. 18 (bottom); Gekko Gallery, p. 19; Leo McGilly, p. 20; Hung Chung Chih, pp. 21, 22 (bottom); Chris W Anderson, p. 22 (top); e X p o s e, p. 23; Tada Images, p. 24; Tutti Frutti, p. 25; Sovfoto/ Getty Images, p. 26; Noppasin Wongchum, p. 27 (Berlin Wall); VCG/ Getty Images, p. 27 (bottom); BOYDKONDERM, p. 28; Everett Collection, Inc./ Alamy, p. 29 (Cloudy With a Chance of Meatballs); Aleksei Kornev, p. 29.